One Crow
A Counting Rhyme

by Jim Aylesworth

illustrated by Ruth Young

J.B. Lippincott New York

One Crow
Text copyright © 1988 by Jim Aylesworth
Illustrations copyright © 1988 by Ruth Young
Printed in the U.S.A. All rights reserved.
1 2 3 4 5 6 7 8 9 10
First Edition

Library of Congress Cataloging-in-Publication Data
Aylesworth, Jim.
    One crow.

    Summary: A farm, first in summer and then winter,
is the setting for counting rhymes from one to ten.
    (1. Counting.   2. Domestic animals—Fiction.
3. Seasons—Fiction.   4. Stories in rhyme)   I. Young,
Ruth, 1946–   , ill.   II. Title.
PZ8.3A95On 1988   (E)   85-45856
ISBN 0-397-32174-0
ISBN 0-397-32175-9 (lib. bdg.)

To All My Darlings at
Hatch School, Oak Park, Illinois,
with Love!

SUMMER

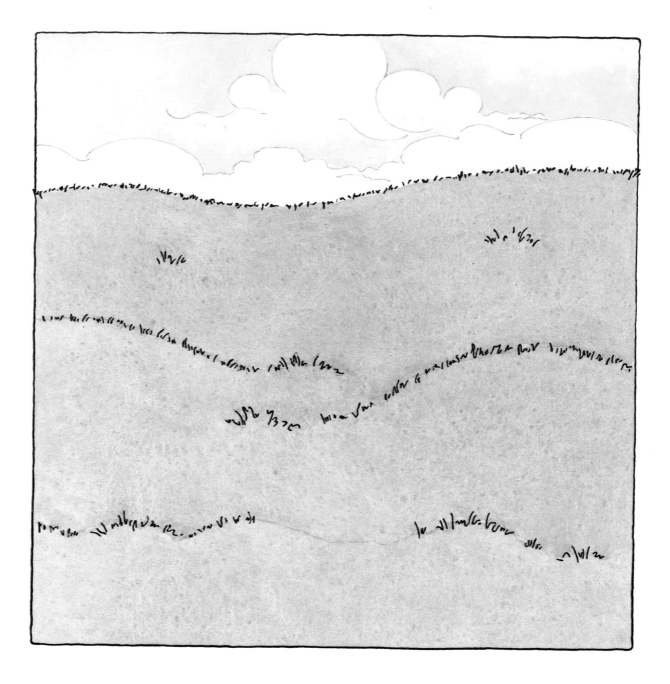

1

One crow sits
on a telephone wire.
Summer sun's up
and climbing higher.

2

Two squirrels chase
in a hollow tree.
Clouds in the sky
are white as can be.

3 Three puppies romp
and wag little tails.
Summer breeze billows
the wash like sails.

4

Four kittens roll
in the tall milkweeds.
Green garden melons
are plump with seeds.

5

Five horses drink
as their tails flip-flop.
Butterflies fly
and grasshoppers hop.

6 Six pigs wallow
in a muddy hole.
Wild berries glisten
like shiny black coal.

7

Seven hens doze
in the soft warm dust.
A broken old plow
is covered with rust.

8

Eight sheep nibble
in the summer green.
Air in the meadow
smells sweet and clean.

Nine cows wander
up the crooked lane.
A barn-roof rooster
is the weather vane.

9

10

Ten children play
on the grassy ground.

going down.

Summer sun's sleepy
and...

WINTER

1

One crow sits
on a telephone wire.
Winter sun's up
and climbing higher.

2 Two squirrels curl
in a hollow tree.
Clouds in the sky
are white as can be.

Three puppies bark
as they run and sniff.
Wash on the line
is frozen stiff.

3

4 Four kittens watch.
They're hunting for mice.
The barnyard puddles
are silver ice.

5

Five horses eat
with heads in a row.
Sunlight sparkles
and snowflakes blow.

6

Six pigs snuggle
in a pile of hay.
Spiderwebs sag,
all dusty and gray.

7

Seven hens nest,
each one in a box.
The old coop's warm
and safe from the fox.

8

Eight sheep huddle
in the winter white.
Air in the meadow
feels crisp and light.

Nine cows wander
up the crooked lane.
A barn-roof rooster
is the weather vane.

9

10

Ten children play
on the snowy ground.

Winter sun's sleepy
and…

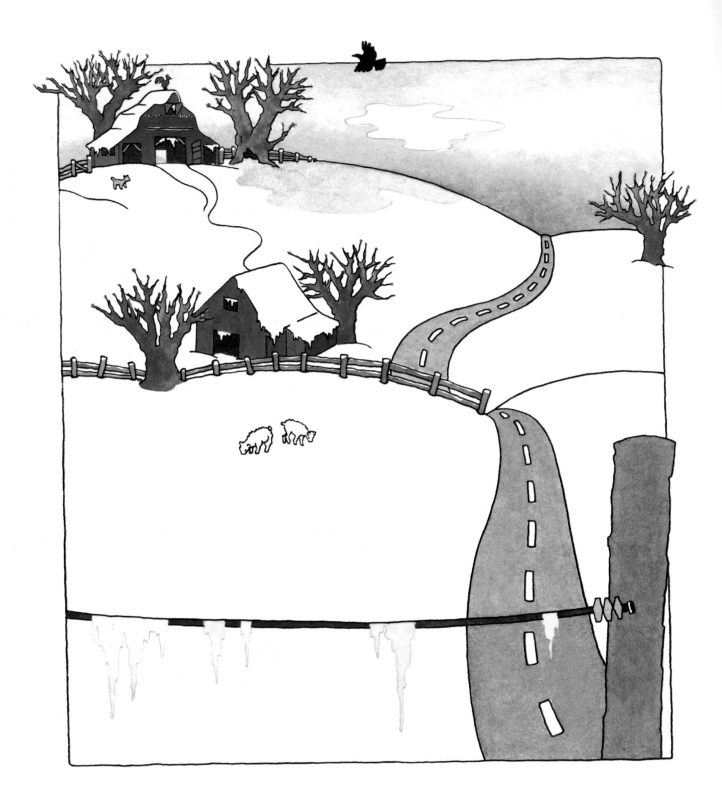

going down.